KALEIDOSCOPE

ROBOTS

by
Darcy Lockman

*B*ENCHMARK *B*OOKS

MARSHALL CAVENDISH
NEW YORK

Series Consultant:
Dr. Paul Benjamin
Pace University
Department of Computer Science and Information Systems

Benchmark Books
Marshall Cavendish Corporation
99 White Plains Road
Tarrytown, NY 10591

Library of Congress Cataloging-in-Publication Data
Lockman, Darcy
Robots / by Darcy Lockman
p. cm. (Kaleidoscope)
Summary: Provides a brief history of robotics, describes tasks for which robots are useful, and suggests future development.
ISBN 0-7614-1047-3
1. Robots—Juvenile literature. [1. Robots.] I. Title. II. Kaleidoscope (Tarrytown, N.Y.)
TJ211.2 L63 2000   629.8'92—dc21   99-058311

Photo research by Candlepants, Inc.
Cover: Image Bank.
Photo credits:Photo credits: Photo Researchers: 4, 6, 10, 13, 18, 21, 25, 29, 30, 33, 34, 38, 40. Corbis: 9, 14, 16, 22. Image Bank: 37.
Sony Corporation: 42.

Printed in Italy

6 5 4 3 2 1

CONTENTS

ABOUT ROBOTS

Robots are machines that can perform human tasks. In the movies and on television they usually look a lot like human beings. But in real life most robots don't look much like us. They can't feel emotion either. *Robots* do make life easier for us, though. What exactly are they?

An android's head under construction. An android is a type of robot that looks like a human being. They are used mostly for entertainment.

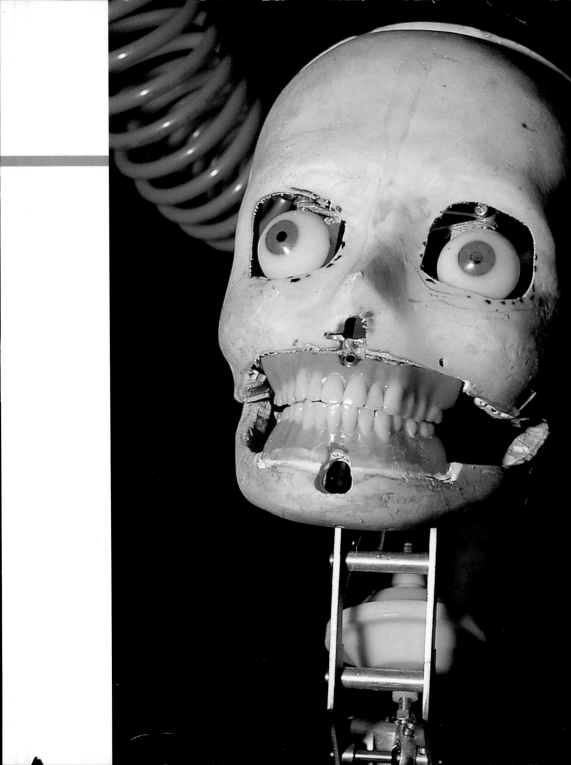

Unlike a computer, a robot can move. This one has legs that allow it to walk and an arm that allows it to place and seal lids on steel drums.

6

WHAT IS A ROBOT?

Have you ever used a computer? A robot has a lot in common with a computer. They are both programmed to perform many different tasks. A computer solves math problems and stores information. A robot, though, does physical labor. Robots can spray paint car parts and assemble engines. They can collect samples of hot gasses from volcanoes. They can locate shipwrecks hundreds of feet below the sea.

Modern robots have *sensors* that allow them to "see," "hear," and "touch" things in the world around them. Of course, sensors aren't as complex as human senses. But they do allow robots to understand when things change around them and to react to those changes.

The study of robots, or *robotics*, is divided into two fields. The first is *robotics engineering*. Robotics engineers design and build robots. The second is the science of robotics. *Robotics science* is not about making robots—it's about studying human actions so that robotics engineers can make better robots.

A robotics engineer works on his creation.

Robotics scientists might watch workers on an auto assembly line to see just how they put together auto parts, or how they move when the assembly belt speeds up. Then robotics scientists can explain the workers' movements to robotics engineers. The engineers will use this information when they create assembly line robots. Without robotics science, robotics engineers wouldn't be able to make such fantastic machines.

These workers are assembling engines at a Honda factory. Robotics scientists will watch what the workers do. Robotics engineers will then design a robot with this information.

ROBOTS PAST AND PRESENT

These hardworking robots haven't been around very long, but people have been building humanlike machines for centuries. In ancient Egypt, priests attached mechanical arms to statues of their gods. The priests would move these arms and claim to be possessed by a god. The Greeks built statues that were moved by water pressure, another effort to convince people that the gods were speaking.

Humanlike machines are no longer used to convince people that the heavens are speaking. This robot, Manny, is used to help research and develop other robots.

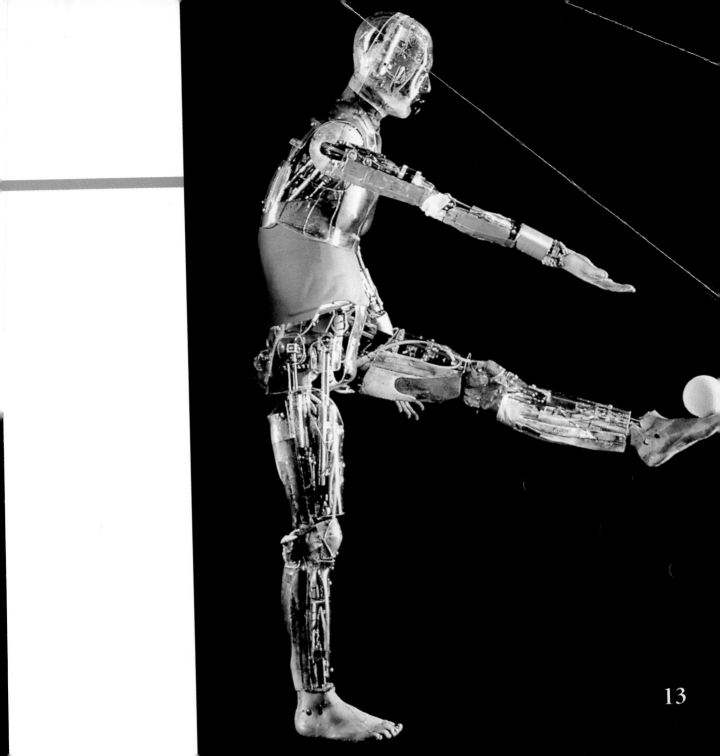

13

In the 1700s, *automata*, or mechanical puppets, were first popular in Europe. Audiences loved to watch the lifelike models of people and animals do things such as writing, drawing, and even playing instruments. In 1801, a loom that could be programmed was invented. These very early robots could do only one thing. They didn't have sensors, so they couldn't react to the world around them.

Mechanical clock figurines, such as this one in Amsterdam, are a form of automata.

The first robots able to sense their environment and respond to it were built in the 1950s in laboratories. In 1950, a scientist named Claude Shannon built a maze-solving mouse. This mechanical mouse was able to find its way through a maze using a computer memory and basic math, making him a bit like a moving calculator.

An early robot, made by General Electric, spins a hula hoop.

GENERAL *GE* ELECTRI

17

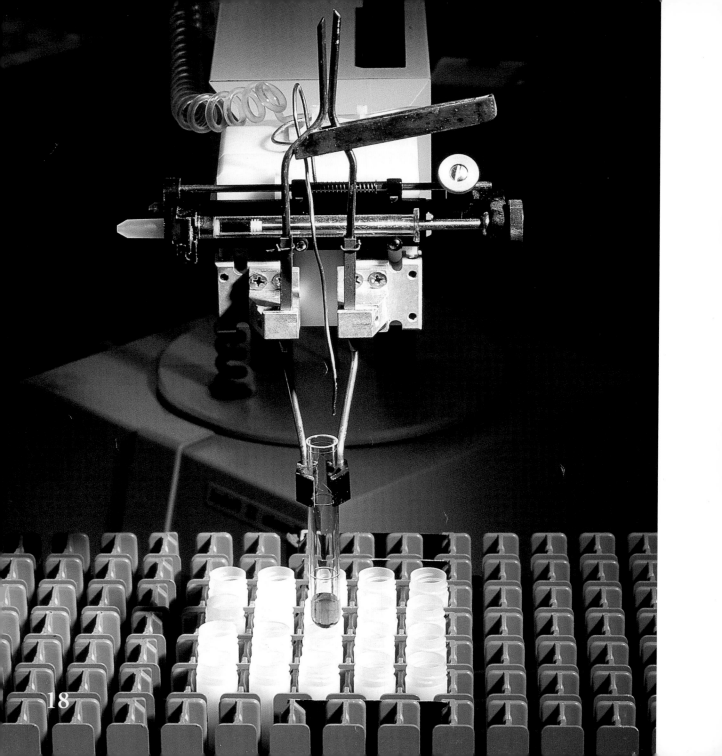

18

Around the same time, Raymond Goertz developed the first *teleoperator*—a machine that could be operated by a human using a remote control. In the same year, General Mills made a machine with a motor that could move objects without any human help. Both Goertz and General Mills kept improving their creations through the next decade.

Robots have become more sophisticated since the 1950s. This robot arm picks up delicate test tubes and gently places them elsewhere for study.

In the 1950s robots started to become practical machines. Twentieth-century inventions such as the computer and sensors were needed, though, before robots could do very complex work.

The computer added memory, which allowed robots to store the instructions they needed to operate. Sensors made the robot truly independent. Before robots had sensors, if there was a large rock in a robot's path, it would just butt up against it until a human came to the rescue. With sensors, the robot could "see" the rock and move around it—all on its own.

Sensors allow this robot to feel the glass and bottle it is holding. Without sensors, it might crush them to bits.

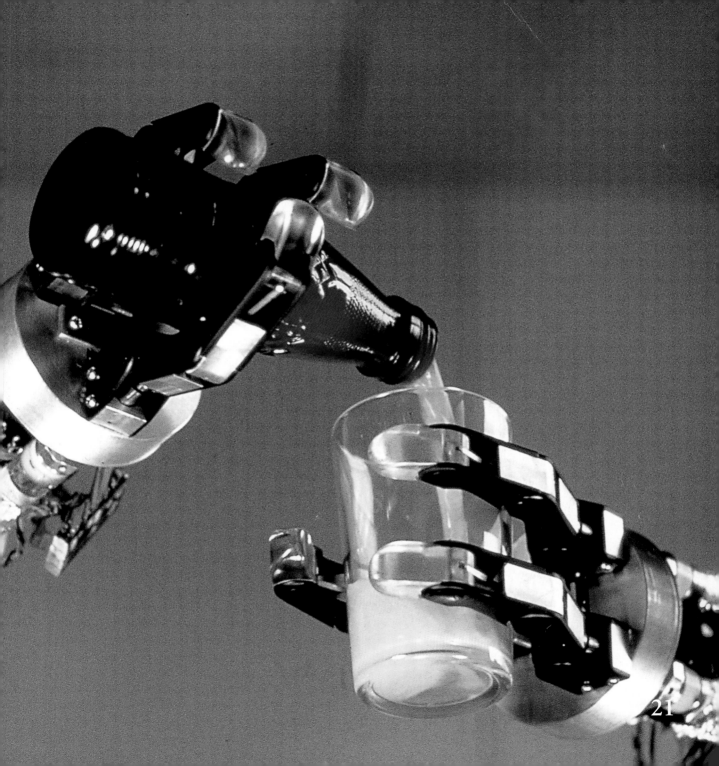

WHAT ROBOTS DO

Robots are used in hundreds of ways. One of the best things about them is that they can be programmed to do dangerous work, jobs that humans have lost their lives doing. One such job is the handling of nuclear materials and radioactive wastes. Robots are not living, so these things cannot harm them.

Robots are used for dangerous work. This police robot is about to pick up a live bomb by remote control.

Robots can also be used in space exploration. Ships are often sent into space without humans on board. Robots on the ships can explore a distant planet's surface. They can do things such as analyze rock and soil samples, read the temperature, and take photographs.

This picture was sent back from Mars by the Mars Pathfinder spacecraft. In the distance, by the large rock called Yogi, *you can see the robot* Sojourner *as it explores the surface of the planet.*

An artist's rendering of a remote controlled robot exploring an ancient shipwreck on the ocean bottom. The robot has cameras that send images to the mother ship.

The sea—dangerous territory, just like space—can be explored by robots, too. Robots can plunge into freezing waters too cold for humans. They can dive to depths that would crush a human being. Without robots, we wouldn't have ever seen some of the strange creatures living on the ocean floor.

Auto factories have also played a big part in the development of robots. Assembling a car involves a lot of boring repetition, something that a robot is well suited for. Robots are good at such jobs because they never get tired and they don't make mistakes out of boredom.

The most common place robots are used is in factories. Here you can see robotic arms welding car frames together.

Robots are not only used in factories. They play a role in all sorts of workplaces. In laboratories they do repetitive work such as arranging test tubes. On farms they've been used to do things like shear sheep.

Robots are used in scientific experiments. This is the first free-swimming robot fish (pictured here with its creator John Kumph). This robot will be used to find out why fish are such great swimmers.

Robots are used in schools to teach computer awareness. They can also help the handicapped power voice-activated wheelchairs. They can feed sick or paralyzed people who can't feed themselves. And robots still have a place as entertainment—you've probably seen toy robots in stores and performing robots in video arcades.

Robots have been developed to help blind people find their way around.

HOW DO ROBOTS WORK?

To understand how a robot works, let's look at one simple task. How does a robot take a car door off of a conveyor belt and place it on a table? In order to pick up a car door, the robot must be able to detect the car door, locate its position, grasp it without damaging it, and place it down in a different spot. It must be able to do this at a certain speed in order to keep up with the pace of the conveyor belt.

This robot's job is to pick up and stack fluorescent lighting tubes. Can you describe how it does this job?

To complete this task, robots need special instructions to guide them. The instructions let the robot know how far to reach it's arm, how tightly to grasp the car door, and where exactly to put it down. A robotics engineer puts these instructions into the robot's memory. This memory is very similar to the memory in a personal computer. Without a memory and a set of instructions, the robot would be like a human body without a brain.

A robotic arm holding a memory chip.

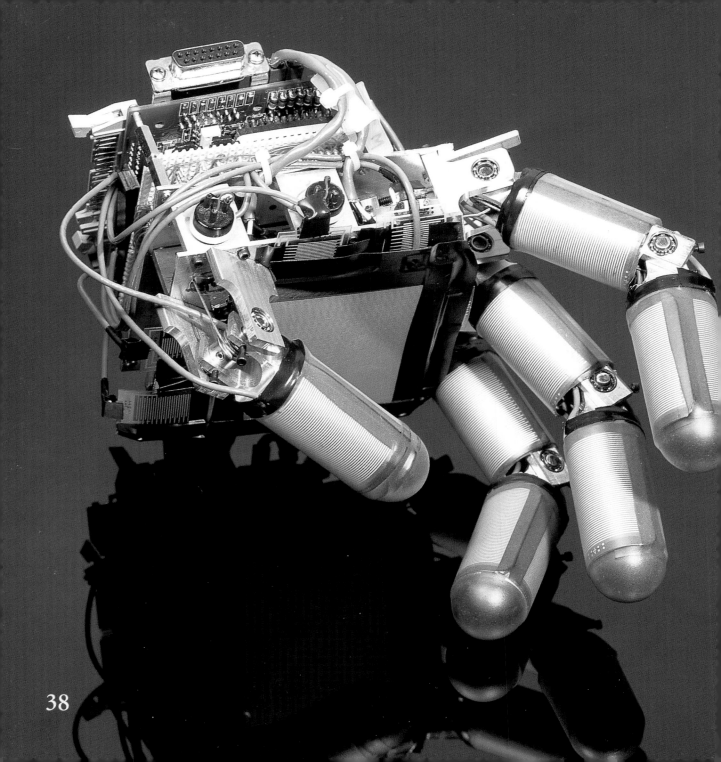

38

A robot's sensors also help it do its job right. They tell the robot if it is holding the car door too tightly or if it is moving too slowly to keep up with the conveyor belt. They also help if anything changes. For example, if the belt stops, the robot's sensors will tell it so and the robot will stop, too.

Robots, of course, do more complex jobs than just picking things up and putting them down. But no matter what the task, memory and sensors are the key.

This is the hand of Cog, *an android developed to study artificial intelligence. Its fingers are covered with a touch-sensitive surface. These surfaces are the robot's sensors.*

ROBOTS IN THE FUTURE

Have you ever seen a movie where robots take over the world? This is a story that has been told many times in science fiction novels, movies, and television shows. In the real world, robots do not —and probably never will do—anything like that. They can't experience emotions as humans can. They don't feel happiness, anger, jealousy, or desire. What that means is that robots will never want to take over the world.

When people get angry, they sometimes want to hurt one another. Because robots don't have the ability to get angry, they will never want to hurt a human being.

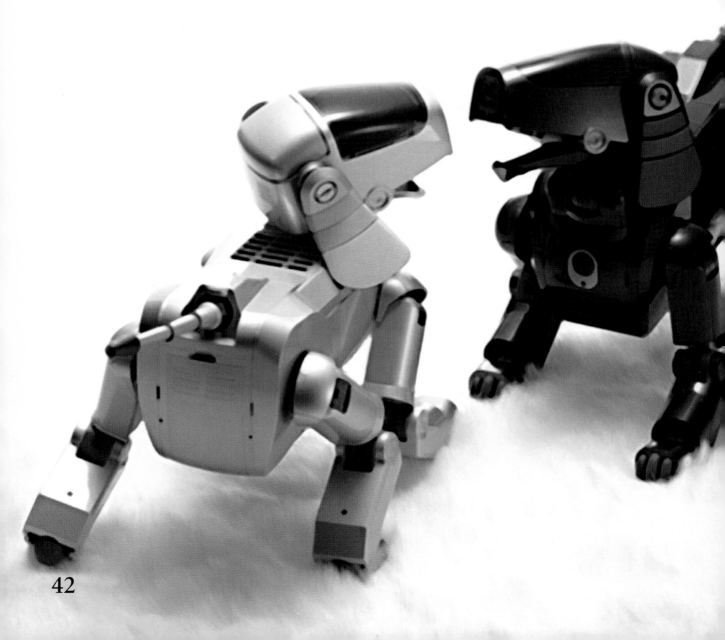

Aibo, a robotic dog made by Sony, can now be ordered from the Internet.

If the future of robots doesn't involve taking over the world, what *does* it hold? As robots become more and more developed, they may play a bigger part in the day-to-day lives of ordinary people. Perhaps we will use them in our homes, for routine tasks such as washing windows and cleaning floors. We may use them in offices, to do things like serve us coffee and sodas. Schools may use them as well, to serve lunch in the cafeteria or to help teachers grade papers. There's really no telling how robots will keep making our lives easier. Maybe one day, you'll have one of your own.

GLOSSARY

Automata   Mechanical puppets. They were built in Europe in the 1700s and were used for entertainment.

Robot   A mobile machine that can be programmed to perform certain tasks.

Robotics   The study of robots.

Robotics engineering   The branch of robotics that deals with designing and building robots.

Robotics science   The branch of robotics that studies how human beings respond to their surroundings in order to make robots that respond in a similar way.

Sensors   Computerized devices that allow robots to detect the location of things.

Teleoperator   A machine like a robot that is operated by remote control.

FIND OUT MORE

Books

Darling, David. *Computers of the Future: Intelligent Machines and Virtual Reality.* Beyond Two Thousand Series. New York: Dillon Silver Burdett Press, 1995.

Fowler, Allan. *It Could Still Be A Robot.* Rookie Read About Series. Danbury CT: Children's Press, 1998.

Skurzynski, Gloria. *Robots: Your High-Tech World.* New York: Simon and Schuster Children's, 1990.

Wickelgren, Ingrid. *Ramblin' Robots: Building a Breed of Mechanical Beasts.* Venture Books series. Danbury CT: Franklin Watts, 1996.

Websites

Get A Grip on Robotics:
http://www.thetech.org/exhibits_events/online/robots/teaser/

Nova Online: Bomb Squad:
http://www.pbs.org/wgbh/nova/robots

The Robot Zoo:
http://www.sgi.com/robotzoo/

San Francisco Robotics Society of America:
http://www.robots.org/

Tech Kids (featuring NASA's robot of the week):
http://www.hompro.com/techkids/

AUTHOR'S BIO

Darcy Lockman is a freelance writer who has written on technology for a number of young adult publications. She lives in New York City.

INDEX

Page numbers for illustrations are in boldface.